PIANO · VOCAL · GUITAR

PAUL McCARTNEY   NEW

ISBN 978-1-4803-6820-0

A Publication of

MPL COMMUNICATIONS, INC.
http://www.mplcommunications.com

Exclusively Distributed By

HAL•LEONARD®
CORPORATION
7777 W. Bluemound Rd. P.O. Box 13819 Milwaukee, WI 53213

Visit Hal Leonard Online at
www.halleonard.com

SAVE US

Words and Music by PAUL McCARTNEY
and PAUL EPWORTH

Driving Pop Rock

I can try to give you ev-'ry-thing you ev - er want-ed,
Got a feel-ing there's a jun-gle rhy-thm beat-ing in me

you're not hard to please. __
when I'm close to you. __

And the on - ly thing I'm
I don't real - ly want to

ask-ing in re-turn is some-thing you can give with ease. __
ask for ma-ny fa-vors but there's some-thing you can do. __

ALLIGATOR

Words and Music by
PAUL McCARTNEY

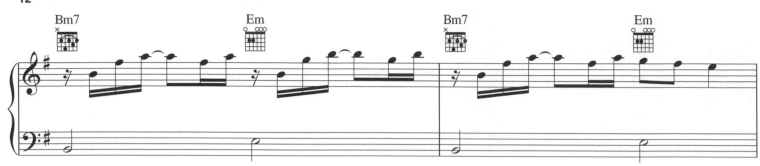

I want some-one who can bail ___ me ___ when I get up to my tricks.

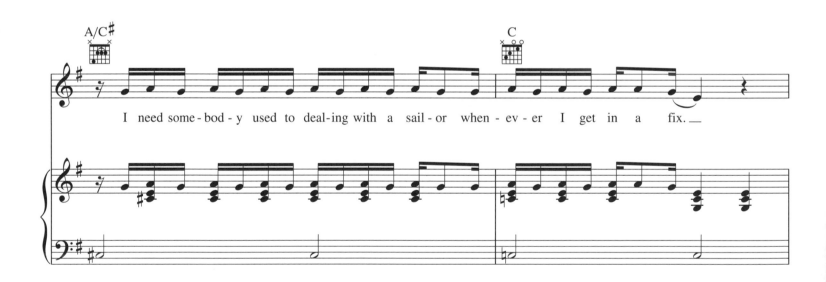

I need some-bod-y used to deal-ing with a sail-or when-ev-er I get in a fix. ___

D.S. al Coda
(take 2nd ending)

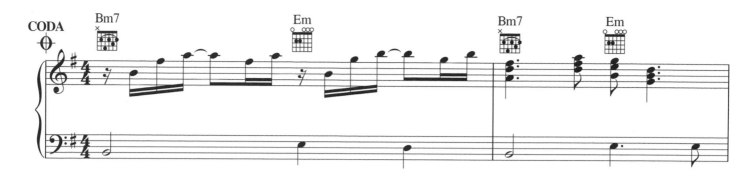

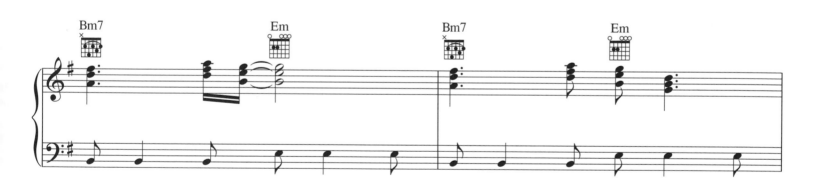

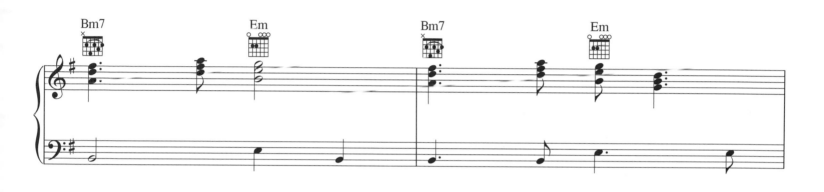

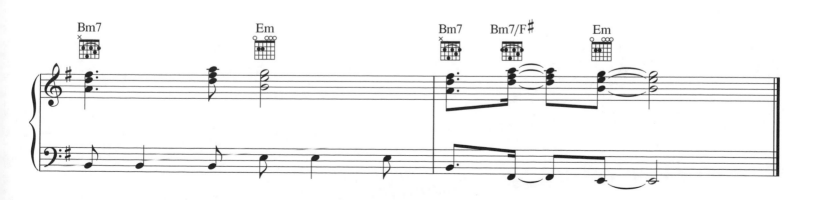

ON MY WAY TO WORK

Words and Music by
PAUL McCARTNEY

Moderate Ballad

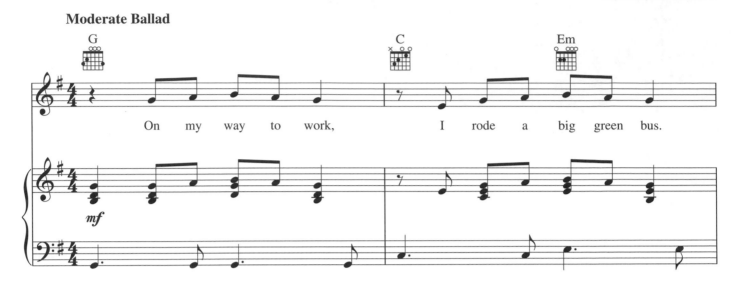

On my way to work, I rode a big green bus.

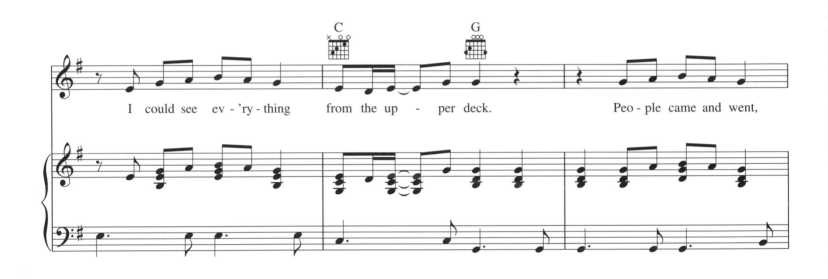

I could see ev-'ry-thing from the up - per deck. Peo - ple came and went,

smok-ing cig - a - rettes. I picked the pack - ets up when the peo - ple left.

On my way to work.

But all the time I

QUEENIE EYE

Words and Music by PAUL McCARTNEY
and PAUL EPWORTH

There were rules you nev-er told me, nev-er came up with a plan. All the sto-ries that you sold me did-n't help me un-der- stand. But I had to get it worked out, had no-bod-y who could

EARLY DAYS

Words and Music by
PAUL McCARTNEY

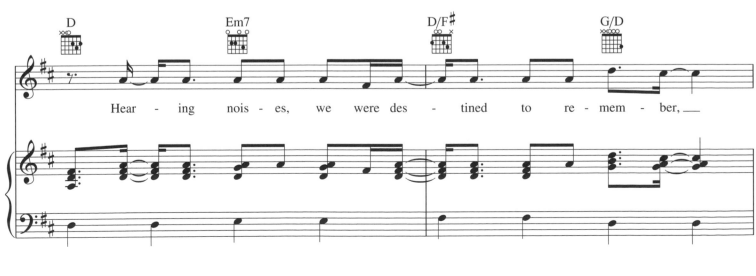

Ooh. _____

Hair slicked back with vas - e - line ____ like the pic - tures on ____ the wall ____

____ of the lo - cal re - cord shop. _____

Hear - ing nois - es, we were des - tined to re - mem - ber, ___

will the thrill____ to nev - er stop. _____

Ooh. _____

Ooh. _____

May sweet mem - o - ries____ of friends from the past____ al - ways

NEW

Words and Music by
PAUL McCARTNEY

Beatle-esque Pop Rock

Don't look at me, ___ it's way ___ too soon ___ to see ___
You came a - long ___ and made ___ my life ___ a song, ___
Don't look at me, ___ I can't ___ de - ny ___ the truth, ___

___ what's gon - na be, ___ don't look ___ at me. ___
___ one luck - y day ___ you came ___ a - long. ___
___ it's plain to see, ___ don't look ___ at me. ___

All ___ my life, ___ I nev - er knew ___ what I could be, ___
Just ___ in time, ___ well I was search - ing for a rock, ___
All ___ my life, ___ I nev - er knew ___ what I could be, ___

APPRECIATE

Words and Music by
PAUL McCARTNEY

D.S. al Coda
(Lyric 1)

EVERYBODY OUT THERE

Words and Music by
PAUL McCARTNEY

Driving Rock

Hey, ev-'ry-bod-y out there, do you know what it's like? If you have-n't got a life, __

give you some of mine. ___ There, but for the

grace of God, ___ go you ___ and I. ___

We're the bright-est ob - jects in ___ the sky. ___

{ Well, }
{ Re - mem - ber, } there, but for the grace of God, ___ go you ___

HOSANNA

Words and Music by
PAUL McCARTNEY

Moderate Ballad

Come now, la - dy, don't you ___ do me wrong. ___ I fell for you and now it ___ ___ won't be long. ___ Be - fore I hold you in my ___ arms, be - fore I take you to my ___ heart a - gain. ___

Recorded a half step lower

I CAN BET

Words and Music by
PAUL McCARTNEY

Lis-ten to me, we can

give it a try, ___ I'll look you straight in the eye ___ and pull you

to me. What I'm gon-na do next I'll leave en-

I've got no plan, yeah, but I'm ___ your man, yeah.

And I'll ___ be there when you're read - y.

LOOKING AT HER

Words and Music by
PAUL McCARTNEY

Moderately

If you

ask her how it's done, she won't know.
haunts me like the sound of the rain

Instrumental

It's like
or a

try'n' to catch the sun on the wa - ter.
riv - er run - ning down to the o - cean.

Instrumental ends

She
I She

ROAD

Words and Music by PAUL McCARTNEY
and PAUL EPWORTH

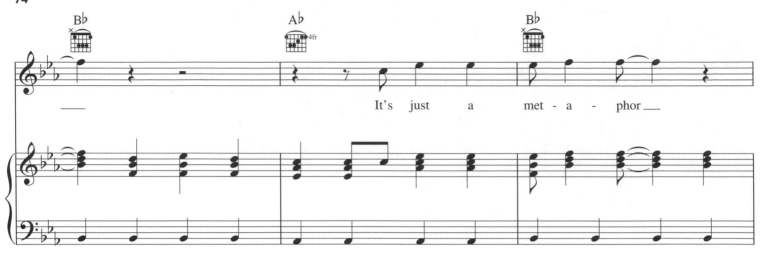

It's just a met - a - phor ___

I use when things ___ aren't go - ing right. ___

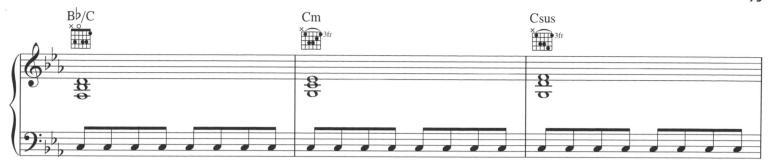

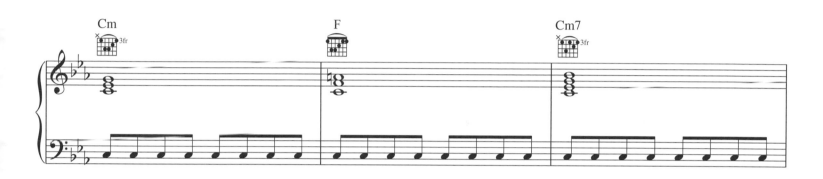

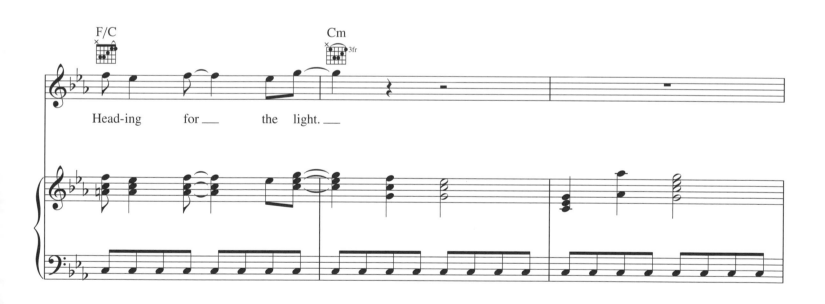

Head-ing   for ___   the light. ___

SCARED

Words and Music by
PAUL McCARTNEY

TURNED OUT

Words and Music by
PAUL McCARTNEY

GET ME OUT OF HERE

Words and Music by
PAUL McCARTNEY

get me out of here.
some-one get me out of here.

Yeah.

Yeah.

Yeah, __

__ when we fight, I don't know __ what to say. __ It feels so bad and yet I

can't run a - way. __ Oh, boy, ___ get me out of here.

Spoken: "I'm a celebrity!"

Some-one get me out ___ of here. ___